The Countries

Sweden

Kate A. Furlong

ABDO Publishing Company

visit us at
www.abdopub.com

Published by ABDO Publishing Company, 4940 Viking Drive, Edina, Minnesota 55435.
Copyright © 2001 by Abdo Consulting Group, Inc. International copyrights reserved in
all countries. No part of this book may be reproduced in any form without written
permission from the publisher.

Printed in the United States.

Photo Credits: Corbis, A/P Wide World

Contributing Editors: Tamara L. Britton and Christine Fournier
Book Design and Graphics: Bob Italia and Neil Klinepier

Special thanks to Helene Suh for her linguistic assistance.

Library of Congress Cataloging-in-Publication Data

Furlong, Kate A., 1977-
   Sweden / Kate A. Furlong.
     p. cm. -- (The Countries)
   Includes index.
   ISBN 1-57765-550-8
    1. Sweden--Juvenile literature. [1. Sweden.] I. Title. II. Series.

DL609 .F7 2001
948.5--dc21

                                                      00-048615

Contents

God dag!

Hello from Sweden! Sweden is in northern Europe. It is nestled between mountains and seas. Swedes enjoy spending time in their beautiful land. Its thick forests are home to many plants and wild animals.

Sweden's government is a **constitutional monarchy**. Its prime minister governs the country. Sweden has a king, but his role is only ceremonial. A **parliament** creates the country's laws.

Sweden has a rich history. It has been home to Viking explorers and rich nobles. Sweden has also produced excellent writers, actors, and scientists.

Sweden has a successful **economy**. Mining and logging are Sweden's main industries. Swedes manufacture goods from these raw products.

Sweden is a strong country. With its beautiful land, solid government, and healthy economy, its future seems bright indeed.

God dag *from Sweden!*

Fast Facts

★ STOCKHOLM

OFFICIAL NAME: Kingdom of Sweden
   (Konungariket Sverige)
CAPITAL: Stockholm

LAND
- Mountain Ranges: Scandinavian Mountains
- Highest Peak: Mount Kebnekaise 6,926 feet (2,111 m)
- Major River: Klar River

PEOPLE
- Population: 8,873,052 (2000 est.)
- Major Cities: Stockholm, Göteborg, Malmö
- Official Language: Swedish
- Religion: Evangelical Lutheran Church of Sweden, Roman Catholicism

GOVERNMENT
- Form: Constitutional Monarchy
- Head of State: King
- Head of Government: Prime minister
- Legislature: Riksdag
- Flag: Blue field with yellow cross extending to edges; short end of cross on mast side
- Other Symbols: Coat of arms with one lion on either side.
- Nationhood: June 6, 1523

ECONOMY
- Agricultural Products: Grains, sugar beets, potatoes, poultry, pork, milk
- Mining Products: Iron ore, copper, lead, zinc, silver, gold
- Manufactured Products: Iron and steel, precision equipment, wood pulp, paper products, processed food, motor vehicles
- Money: Krona (one krona equals 100 öre)

Sweden's flag

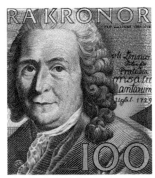

Swedish 100 kronor bill

Timeline

800-1000s	Vikings rule Sweden; Christianity introduced
1350	Black Death kills many Swedes
1611	Gustavus II Adolphus becomes king; leads Sweden in Thirty Years' War
1805-1809	Napoleonic Wars
1975	Sweden passes new constitution

Swedes strolling through a park in Vixby, Götaland Island

Sweden's Rise to Power

Beginning in A.D. 800, Vikings ruled Sweden. They sailed around the world and conquered many lands. Their reign lasted until about A.D. 1000.

Asgar, a French monk, introduced Christianity to Sweden in A.D. 829. But it spread slowly. For 200 years, the Swedes fought many wars over Christianity.

After the Vikings, Sweden was ruled by a series of monarchs and **dynasties**. During the 1200s and 1300s, the noblemen of Sweden often **rebelled** and replaced their rulers. In 1350, many Swedes died during a sickness called the Black Death.

In 1611, Sweden began to expand under King Adolf Gustav II. Sweden fought in the Thirty Years' War. It gained control of new lands. It became a stronger, more independent country.

Opposite page: Vikings sailed in longships, such as the Oseberg Ship, found in Oseberg, Norway.

In the early 1800s, Sweden fought in the **Napoleonic Wars**. After these wars, food was scarce in Sweden. So, thousands of Swedes moved to the United States.

In the 1860s, Sweden's **economy** improved. The country built up its mining, manufacturing, and lumber industries. By 1900, Sweden had become an important industrial nation.

Sweden remained **neutral** in both world wars. It became one of the world's richest countries. The government began using tax money to give all Swedes insurance, hospitals, and schools.

In 1975, Sweden's government passed a new **constitution**. It gave more power to the **parliament** and **cabinet**.

Today, Sweden is important to the world community. The Swedish government belongs to organizations such as the Nordic Council, the United Nations, and the European Union. Through these groups, Sweden gives much to its nation and the world.

Sweden's Prime Minister Goran Persson addresses the United Nations.

Land of the Midnight Sun

Sweden is in Europe. It is on the Scandinavian **Peninsula**. Sweden is mountainous in the north. The land slopes down to plains in the south.

Northern Sweden is called Norrland. It has thick forests and many minerals. It also has Sweden's highest peak, Mount Kebnekaise (KEB-ne-KICE-eh). Sweden's major rivers begin in Norrland's mountains. Though Norrland is Sweden's largest region, few people live there.

Central Sweden is called Svealand (SVEE-ah-LAND). It has plains, hills, and forests. This land is good for farming. Svealand has many lakes, including Lake Vänern (VAN-ern). It is Sweden's largest lake. Svealand is also home to Sweden's capital, Stockholm.

Southern Sweden is called Götaland (YO-tah-land). Parts of southern Götaland have plains with rich soil.

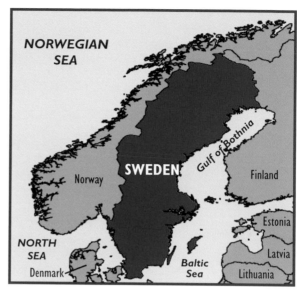

They are Sweden's best farmland. Other parts of Götaland have poor, rocky soil.

Sweden's climate varies from north to south. Northern Sweden has cold, snowy winters and cool summers. Southern Sweden has milder winters and sunny, warm summers. Sweden receives plenty of rain in the summer and fall.

Sometimes Sweden is called Land of the Midnight Sun. In the summer, there is daylight nearly 24 hours a day. But in the winter, there are few hours of daylight. This happens because Sweden is near the **Arctic Circle**.

A river valley in northern Sweden

Rainfall

AVERAGE YEARLY RAINFALL

Inches		*Centimeters*
10 - 20		*25 - 50*
20 - 40		*50 - 100*
40 - 60		*100 - 150*

North
West — East
South

Temperature

Winter

STOCKHOLM

AVERAGE TEMPERATURE

Fahrenheit		*Celsius*
50° - 68°		*10° - 20°*
Under 32°		*Under 0°*
-4° - 14°		*-20° - -10°*

Summer

STOCKHOLM

Wild Things

Swedes have a strong love of nature. That's no surprise, given their beautiful homeland. Swedes respect their land's many types of wild animals and plants.

Northern Sweden is covered with forests. Spruce and pine trees are abundant. Southern Sweden also has forests of beech and oak. Swedes enjoy picking wild berries and mushrooms that grow in the forest.

Sweden's forests are home to all kinds of animals. Northern Sweden is home to bears, owls, and lynx. Some people in northern Sweden raise reindeer. Roe deer, foxes, and hares live all over Sweden. Moose also live in Sweden. There are so many moose that sometimes they cause traffic problems!

The waters around Sweden are rich in wildlife. The Baltic seal, along with cod, mackerel, salmon, pike, and herring live in Sweden's seas. Sweden's waters also attract many birds.

Sweden's great grey owl is one of the world's largest owls. It is over two feet (.6 m) long, and its wingspan is about five feet (1.5 m).

The Swedes

Nearly everyone who lives in Sweden comes from common ancestors. Swedes share a language and religion. They also share physical **traits**. Many Swedes are tall with blond hair and blue eyes.

Sweden also has two native groups. They are the Lapps and the Finns. Both groups live in the north. **Immigrants** also live in Sweden. They come from Europe, Latin America, and the Middle East.

Sweden's official language is Swedish. Nearly all Swedes can read, write, and speak Swedish. Spoken Swedish has a musical sound to it.

Most Swedes belong to the Church of Sweden. It is a Lutheran church. Sweden also has people who are Catholic, Greek Orthodox, and Islamic.

Families are important to Swedes. Most Swedish families are small. In the cities, most families live in apartment buildings.

A Lapp family dancing in traditional clothing

Families often take country vacations. Many families have cottages in the country. They spend time swimming, boating, and relaxing at their cottages.

Swedish families enjoy eating a variety of foods. Sweden is famous for its *smörgåsbord*s. These feasts include cheese, ham, lamb, sausage, and herring. There are also meatballs, stuffed cabbage, and omelets.

Education is free to all Swedish children. The government also provides free books and lunches. Children begin school at age six or seven. Their schools are called *grundskolan* (GRUND-skoo-LAHN). Students learn to read, write, and do math. In third grade, they begin to learn English.

After *grundskolan*, students may continue their education. The next schools are called *gymnasieskolan* (JIM-naw-see-ah-SKOO-lahn). They prepare students for the university or **vocational** school. One out of three Swedes go on to some kind of education after *gymnasieskolan*.

Swedish Meatballs

1 cup sour cream
3 tbsp flour
1/2 tsp dill weed

1 cup water
1 cube beef bouillon
20 cooked meatballs

Mix sour cream, water, flour, bouillon, and dill weed in a saucepan. Cook it over medium heat until well blended and hot. Add meatballs to the sauce. Cook for about 20 minutes. Serve meatballs and sauce over cooked noodles.

AN IMPORTANT NOTE TO THE CHEF: Always have an adult help with the preparation and cooking of food. Never use kitchen utensils or appliances without adult permission and supervision.

English	Swedish
Hello	God dag
Goodbye	Adjö
Please	Var Snäll
Thank You	Tack Så
You're Welcome	Var så god
Yes	Ja
No	Nej

LANGUAGE

A Nation of Wealth

Sweden has a healthy **economy**. This has made it one of the richest nations in Europe. Other countries look to Sweden as an example of a successful economy.

Manufacturing goods is a large part of Sweden's economy. Swedes make machines, ships, chemicals, and paper products. They also make cars, buses, and trucks. Two Swedish carmakers, Volvo and SAAB, have become world famous.

Sweden's forests are another valuable part of the economy. Some trees are used as lumber. Other trees are used to make paper, cardboard, or furniture.

Sweden's land is full of minerals. It is especially rich in iron ore. Swedish people also mine copper, lead, zinc, silver, and gold.

About half of Sweden's energy comes from **hydroelectricity**. The rest is generated by **nuclear** energy.

Farming is a small part of the **economy**. Most Swedish farmers raise animals for milk and other dairy products. Swedish farms also grow grains, sugar beets, and potatoes.

A worker at a Volvo plant in Göteborg, Sweden

Sweden's Cities

Stockholm is Sweden's capital and largest city. It is on Sweden's southeastern coast. The city is built upon 14 islands and part of the mainland. Many bridges connect the islands together.

Stockholm houses Sweden's national government. Most of Sweden's manufacturing takes place there. Stockholm also serves as one of the country's major ports.

Stockholm has many places for its people to enjoy. There are nearly 30 outdoor stages that hold ballets, plays, and concerts. The city's public parks are filled with flowers and sculptures. There is also the Royal Opera, more than 50 museums, and many universities.

Other major cities in Sweden are Göteborg (yeuh-teh-BORJ) and Malmö (MAHL-meuh). Göteborg is on Sweden's southwestern coast. Malmö is on the far southern coast. Both of these cities have important ports. And they are each centers of culture and business.

Stockholm is often called the Venice of the North.

On the Move

Swedes use cars to get from place to place. Most families have at least one car. They drive on the right-hand side of the road, just like in the U.S. and Canada. Sweden has a large system of roads. Thousands of cars use these roads every day.

Sweden also has good public transportation. Buses run in many cities. Stockholm has the world's largest bus system. It has a subway system, too. It is called the *Tunnelbanan* (TOON-el-BAWN-ehn). *Tunnelbanan* stations have become famous for the beautiful artwork displayed in them.

People traveling long distances in Sweden have many choices. They can travel on Sweden's miles of railways. Or, they can fly on Scandinavian Airlines System. It is the airline owned by Sweden, Denmark, and Norway. **Ferries** and boats also connect Sweden with other countries.

Commuter trains cross Stockholm.

The Kingdom of Sweden

Sweden's government is a **constitutional monarchy**. King Carl XVI Gustaf is the head of state. In 1975, Sweden adopted a new **constitution**. It removed all political power from the king. Today, King Carl's role is ceremonial.

The head of Sweden's government is the prime minister. The prime minister is elected by Sweden's **parliament**, the Riksdag. He or she chooses the **cabinet**. It has about 20 advisors in it. Together, they make all government decisions.

Swedish citizens elect the Riksdag's 349 members every four years. Members of the Riksdag pass new laws. They also make the budget and create new taxes.

The taxes in Sweden are some of the highest in the world. Taxes provide Swedes with many benefits. They receive **pensions**, paid sick days, medical care, free education, and paid vacation days.

King Carl and his family at a Nobel Prize ceremony

Time to Celebrate!

Sweden has many holidays and festivals. Swedish holidays mix ancient and modern traditions.

Christmas is the biggest holiday in Sweden. On December 13, young girls dress up as St. Lucia. They wear white robes and a crown of candles. These girls represent the return of summer's long, sunny days.

On Christmas Eve, families decorate a Christmas tree. They also have a *smörgåsbord*. A Christmas **gnome** (nohm) brings children gifts. On Christmas Day, families go to church.

In the spring, Swedes celebrate Easter and Walpurgis (VAHL-burjs) Night. Families celebrate Easter with a dinner of hard-boiled eggs. They also go to church. Walpurgis Night celebrates springtime on April 30. On that night, people hold bonfires and sing songs about spring. Many people attend parties and speeches.

June 19-25 is Midsummer's Eve. It is held during Sweden's longest days. People set up and decorate a maypole. It is a tall cross decorated with flowers and branches. Swedes sing and dance around the maypole.

Swedes in traditional dress dance around maypoles at the Midsummer's Eve celebration.

Sports, Arts, & Inventions

Most Swedes receive about four weeks of paid vacation each year. They usually take their vacations in July. They often travel to a country cottage. While there, they like to take part in many outdoor activities.

In 1910, Sweden created Europe's first national park. Today, Sweden has 26 national parks. These parks provide excellent nature walks, swimming, sailing, and fishing.

Sports are an especially popular **pastime** in Sweden. In the summer, people play tennis and soccer. In the winter, people enjoy skiing, skating, and playing ice hockey.

People in Sweden also appreciate the arts. Sweden has more than 2,000 libraries. One of Sweden's best-loved authors is Astrid Lindgren. She wrote a series of children's books about Pipi Longstocking. They have won countless medals and awards.

A skier at the World Cup Alpine Championships, held in Sweden

People also enjoy attending the theater and movies. The leading theater is the Royal Dramatic Theater in Stockholm. It has been giving performances since 1788. In recent times, Sweden has made an impact on American movies. Famous Swedish actors include Greta Garbo, Ann-Margret, and Ingrid Bergman. Sweden's Ingmar Bergman is a world-famous director.

Sweden is also known for its crafts. The county of Dalarna (DAH-lah-nah) is known for wooden crafts. These include tables, chests, and small carved objects. The county of Småland (SMOW-land) is known for its glass crafts. It is home to the world-famous Orrefors (OR-re-FORSH) company, which makes beautiful glasses, vases, and bowls.

Many kinds of music can be heard in Sweden, from classical to rock. Swedish folk music is very popular. It began in the Middle Ages. Fiddles and accordions accompany the music. Today, Swedes still enjoy singing these folk songs.

Villagers play folk music at a local festival.

Swedish artists and musicians have given much to the world. Swedish scientists have, too. They have invented items still used today. For example, Swedish scientists invented the zipper, safety matches, and the Celsius thermometer.

One of Sweden's most important inventors was a man named Alfred Nobel. He patented more than 300 inventions. His most famous invention was **dynamite**. Nobel created an award for other great scientists, writers, and inventors. It is called the Nobel Prize.

Over its long history, Sweden has built a strong country. Its government and **economy** have been shining examples for other countries. Its rich **traditions** have created a strong bond among the country's people. As Sweden marches forward, its people have a bright future ahead of them.

The sons of Professor Ferid Murad, winner of the 1998 Nobel prize for chemistry, try out the royal family's chairs.

Glossary

Arctic Circle - an imaginary line that runs through the north pole. In the Arctic Circle, the sun never rises on the shortest day of winter and the sun never sets on the longest day of summer.

cabinet - the group of advisors to Sweden's prime minister.

constitution - the laws that govern a country.

constitutional monarchy - a form of government with a king or queen. He or she must follow the laws of the constitution.

dynamite - a powerful explosive.

dynasty - a family who rules a country for many generations.

economy - a system of managing the production, distribution, and consumption of goods and services.

ferry - a boat used to carry people, goods, and cars across a body of water.

gnome - a dwarf that appears in Swedish folk tales. Legends say it guards the earth's treasures.

hydroelectricity - electricity produced by water-powered generators.

immigrant - a person who comes into a foreign country to live.

Napoleonic Wars - a series of wars fought in Europe from 1800 to 1815. Sweden was involved in the wars from 1805-1809.

neutral - a country that takes neither side in a war.

nuclear - of or relating to atomic energy.

parliament - the highest lawmaking body in Sweden.

pastime - something that amuses and makes time pass pleasantly.

peninsula - land that sticks out into water and is connected to a larger land mass.

pension - a regular payment given to someone. Usually pensions are earned through long service at a job.

rebel - to resist or disobey authority.

tradition - something that has been passed down from one generation to the next.

trait - a quality that distinguishes one person or group from another.

vocational - of or relating to training in a skill or trade to be pursued as a career.

Web Sites

Swedish Information Smörgåsbord
http://www.sverigeturism.se/smorgasbord

This site is the world's largest English-language source for information about Sweden. It includes facts about Swedish provinces, nature, culture, lifestyles, society, and industry.

This site is subject to change. Go to your favorite search engine and type in "Sweden" for more sites.

Index